AF472396

J. BERT FREEMAN

# YOUR Positive Direction NOW

*Skills and approaches you can use immediately to handle life's realities*

BOOKS
By J. Bert Freeman

*Taking Charge of Your Positive Direction*
*Your Positive Direction NOW*

SEMINARS AND COURSES
By J. Bert Freeman and T.A.L.K. Associates

Titles:
*Above the Clouds: The Positive Directions of Your Attitude*
*Consistent Positive Direction™ Core Development Course*
*Consistent Positive Direction Practitioner Course*
*Consistent Positive Direction* ***RPM*** *Course*
*—(**R**elationships, **P**erformance and **M**orale) Working Together*
*Positive Direction Presentation Skills Course*
*How to Exercise Complete Respect in a Positive Direction*
*Peanut Butter and Jelly*
*The Positive Directions of Data*
*RPM Leadership Programs*
*The Silent Mentor*
*Silent Mentor Leadership*
*Unity of Effort in a Positive Direction™*
*Whole Brain Positive Direction*
*Excellence on the Same Page*
*Workplace Respect*

# YOUR POSITIVE DIRECTION NOW

*Skills and approaches you can use immediately to handle life's realities*

J. BERT FREEMAN

Printed in the United States of America

ISBN 978-0-557-36040-6

# CONTENTS

# INTRODUCTION

How does what we say today impact our lives tomorrow? Our choice of words can move us in a direction toward or away from effective personal and professional relationships and we are in charge of that choice. Positive direction means that the words we speak steer us toward the successes or outcomes that we want or need with others. After years of developing programs and processes called *Consistent Positive Direction*™, this book identifies the core skills and approaches that you can use right away to handle those important relationships.

*Consistent Positive Direction* is described as speaking, writing, learning and impacting reality toward the goals, achievements, results, accomplishments or outcomes that really matter. These skills and approaches came from learning, developing and teaching ways to interact successfully with others, *when what we have to say really matters*. Chapters 1 and 2 provide you with the know-how to use the sentence to sentence skills of *Consistent Positive Direction*, called Verbal Positive Approach™. You will understand how the choice of words that you speak can either keep you away from or move you closer to where you need to be. I encourage you to participate in the skill exercises to accelerate your learning and understanding. Verbal Positive Approach helps you to stay consistent in talking toward what you want or need for your life and the lives of others. I call it the language of Consistent Positive Direction.

Chapter 3, "Above the Clouds – The Positive Directions of Your Attitude", teaches how you can express any attitude in a positive direction, whatever your feelings. You learn the impact your abilities for respect, listening and learning have on taking your attitude above the clouds. It introduces you to the power of using these skills and approaches that goes beyond adjusting words and sentences. Best of all you can use what you learn immediately.

In this book, skills and approaches are shared that can be valuable to you in your everyday life and special situations and circumstances. It contains choices and alternatives that expand your options for interacting with others. However, it is written with the absolute acknowledgment that *you can take charge of what you say and write,* when it really matters. Read, learn and enjoy.

# Chapter 1

## Consistent Positive Direction

Welcome. You are about to enter a new dimension of human interaction that can start you on a lifelong trek of forward movement in your personal and professional relationships, in your high aspirations and in your everyday life. So often our perceptions, feelings and attitudes get in the way of what we want to accomplish. This book will teach you the core of the skills and approaches that empower you to *take charge* of your interactions in ways that can create successful outcomes. I call it Consistent Positive Direction. The description of Consistent Positive Direction includes skills and approaches to speak, write, learn and impact reality in the *direction* of the required and desired outcomes, results, accomplishments, achievement, goals, objectives and/or successes.

Many people try to concentrate on 'being positive.' While being positive is important, it is only part of the answer. Whether I am speaking or writing, I have to *consistently* express myself in the *direction* of the success that needs to be achieved. I have to *consistently* express myself in the *direction* of the progress that needs to be made. I have to *consistently* express myself in the *direction* of the goals that need to be accomplished. I have to *consistently* take what I learn and translate it into expressing the opportunities, or the encouragement, or the leadership, or the respect that is required to move forward.

You probably have your own perception about the meaning of positive direction. When I tell people that I teach Consistent Positive Direction, some say, "That means that the glass is half full, right?" In response I say, "If you want a full glass, then the positive direction *is* half full. If you want an *empty* glass, the positive direction is half empty." A few years ago, I was driving a van across a one-way bridge in Philadelphia. All of the 5 lanes on the bridge were traffic lanes.

Narrow sidewalks were the only spaces between the outside lanes and the sides of the bridge. There were two approaches that merged onto the bridge. I drove onto the bridge from the right approach. A few seconds later, my vehicle stopped moving forward. It was my transmission. I tried other forward gears, but discovered reverse was the only gear working. A few yards behind me was a small median just between the two approaches as they merged onto the bridge. It looked like it was wide enough and long enough for the van. As soon as there was a break in the traffic, I quickly and carefully backed the van onto the median. It just fit. So in that situation, for me, the positive direction was reverse.

Positive direction, then, can be a full glass or an empty glass, forward or reverse, up or down, one side or the other, whatever direction it takes for you to reach your destination.

**Which way is positive direction?**

**Half Full/Half Empty; Forward/reverse?**

All of us have one or a number of compelling demands on our lives. We want our relationships to be better. Of course, we want to be in a better financial situation, and have more harmony in the workplace, in our neighborhoods, and in our schools. Take a minute and think of the most compelling demand on your life in which something *must* change; it must get better.

This "thing" faces you everyday. It has become such a reality that you want to talk about it to anyone who will listen. You want to find someone who identifies with what you are saying. You are compelled to go on and on about the things that are happening to you and detail how other people are part of the cause. You want someone to say, "Yes, I know what you mean…" and be on your side every word of the way. Well, as much as you want to talk about your current situation, will that move you forward? Sometimes, the process of change begins with you and you can start that process right away. Simply change the *direction* of what you've been saying. Talk *toward* the required and desired outcomes, results, accomplishments, achievements, goals, objectives and/or successes that you want—the *positive direction.*

Many people say that they tried being positive when change was needed. In some situations they say, "I've tried being nice. *This is reality.*" However, the best approach toward changing reality is to *understand* it.

## Reality

To really understand reality, it is important to know that there are two (2) parts to reality; one is the current reality and the other is the reality that needs to be in place. Many times the current reality can be so intense that it consumes all of your time and energy, especially your speaking energy.

For example, we often hear the phrase "Stop the violence." When you say, "Stop the violence," you continue to talk about the very thing that you are trying to 'get away from.' You are still talking about the current reality instead of the reality that you want. What do you really want? You want peace; you want safe schools; you want safe and comfortable neighborhoods. Talk that way. If you spend 95% of your speaking energy on the current reality, how much is left for the future? Yes, only 5 percent. You end up spending most of your time and energy talking about the very things that you want to 'get away from,' instead of the things that you want to 'move toward.' Determine the reality that you want, then put 95% of your speaking energy in *that* direction. Have you, or someone that you know, ever expressed an idea and the response was, "Get real!" That kind of response encourages you to talk longer about what's happening now. Instead, you can help everyone to understand that you *are* being real. You *are* facing reality. You just want to put your energy, especially your speaking energy, into the reality that needs to take place.

The best start that you can make to cause change in your life (impact reality in a positive direction) is to put your speaking energy into the reality that you want. That way, you will get more help. You will create more ways for people to support your new efforts. Yes, you will *create*. It is easy to predict what will happen to you tomorrow when you operate from yesterday's information and yesterday's feelings. Peter Drucker once said, "The best way to predict the future is to *create* it…" That future starts with the words that come out of your mouth. If you want peace, talk peace; if you want success, talk success; if you want trust, talk trust.

There are three approaches that will help to move you closer to the reality that you want or need:

- The Starting Line
- The Start Options
- The PC Upgrade

Consider your current reality as your **'Starting Line'**. Whether you are in a race or just exercising, when you get to the starting line there is only one place you go – Forward. Establish the circumstances of any situation as your starting line and move forward from there.

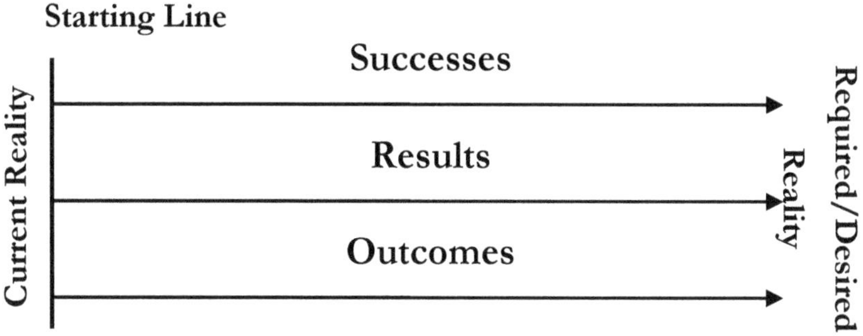


Positive Direction = Forward Movement and Continuous Improvement

I call the sentence-to-sentence way to handle reality the "**Start Options**." Talk about what needs to *start* instead of what needs to stop; talk about what needs to be in place, what needs to be happening. At times, you might need more time to decide what needs to start. If so, then say that you need more time. Say it to yourself and anyone else. Even that is a good start.

Like computers, people need **PC Upgrades**. When we talk about what needs to 'start,' we are giving ourselves a PC Upgrade. The 'P' stands for Predicting. We can easily predict what will happen, if we think of the future in relation to present and past circumstances. If we say something like "They don't care and they never will" or "They will never change," we are probably stating our feelings based on present and past information. We are probably talking more about what needs to 'stop,' than what needs to 'start.' If everything remains the same and we talk the same way, then circumstances will probably continue as we predicted. That, of course, gives us the wonderful luxury of 'being right.' We will be able to say, "See! I told you" and, of course, we love to be right.

The 'C' stands for 'Creating.' You begin to create the circumstances that you want when you talk about what needs to start. You talk into new or different territory. You talk about moving toward a goal or result, rather than getting away from present and past circumstances. For example, when we say, "Stop the violence," we are saying "Get away from violence." When we say, "Let's always be peaceful" we are talking toward the results that we really want. That is a major step in creating peace. Oftentimes, when you talk to create the desired or required future or results, you influence others to talk that way also. If it sounds too soft, *insist* on it, putting every ounce of your speaking energy toward creating the future.

For example, if you have to have various committees, rather than having a committee on what needs to stop, like 'violence,' have a committee on 'peace.' Rather than having a committee on 'racism,' have a committee on 'racial equity. Rather than having a committee on 'sexual harassment,' have a committee on 'gender respect.' If you are in a meeting, and someone asks, "What went wrong?" you can ask "What needs to be right?" Each of us has tremendous power to effect change in a positive direction, simply by speaking in a positive direction. Of course, I recognize that people have jobs or assignments with the specific responsibility of asking, "What went wrong?" There are times that we have to ask, "What happened?"

You may have many opportunities to use the Start Options. In the workplace, for example, there is so much that people say "has got to stop." Well, if something has to stop, something has to start. So, talk that way. Talk about the respect that has to start, instead of the "disrespect" that exists. Talk about the teamwork that has to start, instead of the 'lack of teamwork' that has to stop. Talk about the fairness that has to start, instead of the 'favoritism' that has to stop. Talk about the trust that has to start, instead of the 'mistrust' that has to stop. When addressing workplace performance, talk about increasing the frequency of 'completing orders' or 'shipping orders on time,' instead of talking about stopping the frequency of 'incomplete orders' or 'late shipments.'

In education, we are embarking on quests to significantly increase the academic performance of our school aged children. Talk that way. Talk about the *higher attendance* that has to start, instead of the truancy that has to stop. Talk about the behavior that has to *start*, instead of the behavior that has to *stop*. Talk about *graduation rates*, instead of 'dropout rates.' Talk about the *peer support* that has to start, instead of the peer pressure that has to stop. Talk about the *respect* that children must exercise, instead of stopping the *disrespect*. Instead of speaking or writing to predict academic *failure* (what you want to get away from), talk to *create* or *assure academic 'success'* (what you want to move toward). Everyone can do that. Change the language to change the direction.

## The Opportunity Models for Action (An Overview)

The Opportunity Models for Action is an essential part of Consistent Positive Direction that you can use everyday. They are:

1. Talk or influence *toward* the outcome that needs to occur.
2. Communicate to DO instead of to 'don't.'
3. Build allies in the direction of success, instead of perpetuating differences.
4. Talk about what you are FOR.
5. **C**ontribute **Y**our **I**nput in a positive direction (**CYI**) in a way that you add to an effort rather than take away from the effort.
6. Exercise Complete Respect in a positive direction.
7. Empathize in a positive direction.

The Opportunity Models involve your interaction with others, whether it is everyday conversation, formal discussions or dialogue, teaching, or raising children. *You can speak to everybody in a positive direction.* Imagine being able to use these essentials all of the time—in any circumstance, and in any situation. With practice, you can get to the place where these skills become automatic. When you use them all of the time, you speed up your progress; you create more allies; you also create the environment that you need for success. You stir up the energy that moves things forward and gets things done.

Think about when you are driving; you use your turn signals to change lanes. It seldom takes more than one person to let you in, because you are indicating what you want to do. Just as you use your turn signals in driving, you can use your turn signals when you speak, and when you write, such as filling out an application, when you are asked, "What do you want to accomplish?" Sometimes gaining allies is as simple as telling people what you want to accomplish or talking about your goals. An ally can be anyone who can help you whether it is a friend or otherwise. *You* are a powerful source for gaining the allies that you need. It is consistency that makes the Opportunity Models for Action work best. You can use them, immediately, in any situation, under any circumstance.

**1. Talk or influence *toward* the outcome that needs to occur.**

In one of my leadership sessions, a participant said, "the opposite of 'talking toward' is like driving and always looking in the rear view mirror, rather than keeping your eyes on where you are going." The best way to get to where you want to go is to keep your eyes in that direction; keep your speaking and your writing in that direction. Many people have expressed how the human body is made for forward movement.

Something that a minister said once had a strong impact on me. He described how our eyes are focused forward; our ears are bent forward; our noses are pointed forward; even the sounds from our mouths travel forward. Human beings, he concluded, are built for forward movement. In fact, he said, "we should be mindful that all of the openings in the human body are forward except one." That may be important to remember when there is a lot of talk about what to 'get away from.' So, you are living proof that you are designed for forward movement and *positive direction.*

**2. Communicate to DO.**

When you give instructions, give DO instructions instead of 'don't' instructions; set up DO plans; develop a DO strategy; run a DO campaign. Tell your children what you want them to *do*. For example, tell them to "come in before 9:00" rather than "don't stay out after 9:00." You can be just as firm and just as insistent. Your message will still be clear.

**3. Build allies in the direction of success, instead of perpetuating differences.**

When you want to gain allies, you can certainly use your turn signals. However, when you want active participants, you have to ask for help or tell them what you want them to do. Then it is important to be invitational instead of confrontational.

Some people want to be your allies; they want to actively help and support you. Some people *have to* be your allies, whether they want to or otherwise. Invite them both into your positive direction. It is *your* direction. So you have the luxury of telling them the support that you need. Therefore, you *can* be invitational. Sometimes, when you think people are in your way, you act like they are in your way then you tell other people that they are in your way. Often you are ruled by your perception, before anything happens. You can put the same amount of energy into making someone an ally as you do in holding on to your differences.

**4. Talk about what you are FOR.**

When you want to take a stand, express your reasons in a positive direction. Examine your compelling demand. You have every reason to justify your position. However, instead of saying something like, “That’s not fair!” when you are talking about that particular situation, talk about what needs to be fair. If you think it’s too weak, then *insist* on it. Sometimes you will have to make yourself think and talk about what is fair. Let the ‘fairness’ that you want become a part of you. If you are *for* fairness, talk that way.

**5. Contribute Your Input in a positive direction (CYI) in a way that you add to an effort.**

I define CYI as Contributing Your Input in a positive direction. You always have opportunities to speak in a way that you contribute to a situation, rather than take away from it. You can talk about what can be improved or made better. You can talk more about what can move things forward, than what will hold things back. Even in your own compelling situations, you can use CYI to stay focused.

In 1996, one of my daughters wanted to apply for a scholarship at a particular university and needed to submit her paperwork by a certain date. I assumed that she would handle everything. The due date was on a Saturday. On the Friday night before, when I asked her if she had turned in her scholarship application, she said, “No.” That’s when I found out that it *was* due the next day. Since she was already on the campus spending the night with a friend, she said that she would take it to the admissions office the next morning.

When she got there, she discovered that the office was closed. She called and told me the situation. I really wanted to ask her, "Why did you wait so long!" Instead, I took the opportunity to contribute to the situation. I said, "I will come to pick you up and we will try to find a way."

After I picked her up, we went back to the admissions office. I walked up to the door myself and it was indeed locked. Just as I walked away, a woman passing by saw me and said, "Can I help you?" I explained the circumstances and told her how important it was for my daughter to turn in her scholarship application immediately. She said that the admissions office was usually closed on Saturday. Just as I was walking away, the woman said to me, "Wait a minute; I used to work here and I might still have a key." She looked into her purse and found a key to the building. She acknowledged the urgency and took the application and assured me that she would take it to the appropriate office inside. I said, "Thank you very much!" She apparently got the application in the right hands, because my daughter received a full scholarship from that university. Four years later, my daughter graduated and she was also selected as the outstanding woman of the university for her graduating class.

That was a compelling demand for my daughter and me. So by contributing my input in a positive direction, by simply saying, "We'll try to find a way," rather than lecturing her about waiting so long to turn in the application, I helped to move things forward.

When you use CYI, you will talk about the improvements that are needed; you will generate ideas that focus you forward. When you see that you only have so much time to do something, you can talk about utilizing the time that you *do* have. You *may* be involved in the compelling circumstances of someone else. If so, you can use CYI to ask questions. You can identify and state the changes that need to be made.

Using the same example about time, if someone says, "I don't have enough time," you can say, "Let's work with the time that you do have and see how it can be increased." When you contribute your input in a positive direction (CYI), you add to the effort.

**6. Exercise Complete Respect in a positive direction.**

Treat people with respect, anyway. Many times when we have strong differences of beliefs or opinions with people or we want to make people pay for what they did to us, we feel that we have a 'perfectly good right' to say anything that we want to them, *and/or* about them. We even go as far as getting other people and friends on our side. Sometimes those feelings are so strong, that it would probably take more than anything that I could tell you for you to exercise complete respect anyway.

I've also been in situations in which I wanted to make someone pay for what they did to me so much that I felt perfectly justified saying anything that I wanted to them and doing everything that I could to get others to feel the same way. However, as I learned more about respect, I realized how much I was in control.

Respect is a strong part of building relationships or establishing what needs to happen or be in place. If you have a rule of only respecting those who respect you, you limit the opportunities to bring the best out of people. However, if you always exercise respect for everyone whatever the circumstances, you set yourself up to take advantage of the creativity and productive decision-making that moves things forward. When you label people, you *look* for the label that you give them. If you call someone 'selfish,' for instance, you may recognize the selfishness in that person enough to hide other qualities or motives that may help you. Take the label away. Instead of saying someone is selfish, say that he/she needs to be more considerate. You are the center for respect to work in a positive direction.

**7. Empathize in a positive direction.**

Expressing empathy simply means to acknowledge that you understand or identify with someone's circumstances. You can just as easily acknowledge what the person wants to 'move toward' as you can acknowledge what the person wants to 'get away from.' You may know someone who has a 'compelling demand' in his life. For example, he may need to be in a better financial position and you want to express empathy for him. So, be empathetic in a positive direction. You can say, "I know that you want your finances in order" instead of "I know what it is like to be *broke*." If you have a 'compelling demand' in your own life, be empathetic to yourself in a positive direction. You know you want to move forward from where you are now. Then talk in that direction. Talk toward the required or desired results. The words you speak when expressing empathy, position you at the center for influencing movement in a positive direction.

That was a brief overview of The Opportunity Models for Action. You can learn about them in more depth in the book *Taking Charge of Your Positive Direction* (Freeman 2006).

In the late 1960's and during the '70's, I was a competitive fencer. One of my coaches was Steve Bushnovsky. Steve emphasized to me, with his strong Hungarian accent, that after I learn a skill, to "make it a part of your individual self." That is one of the things that helped me to become a U.S. National Champion and Olympian in 1972.

As you learn these skills, you can make Consistent Positive Direction "a part of your individual self." If you feel as though you are being extra nice, stop yourself and go back to being the same person that you were 5 seconds ago. Keep your personality; keep your savvy. If you feel that you need a personality shift, you may want to go to a 'personality shift' workshop. Yet, as you increase your knowledge and use of these skills, you will experience the silent power of this work. You will know that this can be one of the answers to interact successfully with others.

## Start Right Away

Now, carry out this simple task. It will only take a short time. You probably have started already. Remember that you were asked to determine the most compelling demand on your life in which a change must occur. Write it down then consider these actions in your speaking. Be consistent.

1. Using your compelling demand as your **'starting line'**, State the reality that you want, in a positive direction. Then, talk that way. For instance, you may feel that you want more respect. You could say, "I want people to respect me from now on" instead of "I don't want to be disrespected anymore."

2. Develop **'Start Options'** by stating what needs to *start* for the respect that you want. For example:

- I want people to use respectful language around me.
- I want people to acknowledge my opinions.
- I want my children to keep the house neat, all of the time.
- I want people to recognize me as an individual.

3. Using the **'PC Upgrade'** Start creating, in a positive direction, the circumstances *necessary* for respectful behavior toward you

to improve. You can at least change the things that are in your control. For example:

- Make sure that you are also respectful to others.
- Examine what you say. Even if you feel that what you have been saying is okay, there may be other useful changes that you can make.
- Let others know what you are trying to accomplish in your life, on your job or with your family.

1. Write the reality you want, using your compelling demand as your starting line.

________________________________________________

________________________________________________

________________________________________________

________________________________________________

2. Write what needs to start for the reality that you want or need.

a.

b.

c.

3. Start creating, in a positive direction, the circumstances necessary for your *required* or desired reality to exist.

a.

b.

c.

When you handle your most compelling demand consistently with just the information shared above, you will recognize that the improvements you want will start to occur. *You are the center*. So, take charge of *your* positive direction.

A few years ago, my sister said to me that as you use the language of Consistent Positive Direction, “You are in charge.” I liked that phrase and I used it from the perception that, in any situation, you are in charge. After recent years of developing more accurate knowledge of the skills that you are about to learn, I finally understand. It simply means that you are in charge of *your own positive direction*, in any situation, and under any circumstance.

# Chapter 2

## The Core Skills: *Verbal* Positive Approach

*Verbal Positive Approach includes skills to interact in a positive direction whenever you speak or write, from the time you get up in the morning to the time you go to sleep at night, in any situation, under any circumstances whether face-to-face or out of sight.* Verbal Positive Approach is the core; it makes 'Consistent Positive Direction' consistent.

In 1986, I created and began sharing the skills of Verbal Positive Approach. It was the beginning of a fascinating journey. Little did I know that those skills would be so important. Even in our computer age, when digital systems work at lightening speed to provide information and to develop decisions, the Consistent Positive Direction within each of us can work at that same speed, all day, everyday.

Verbal Positive Approach makes your 'positive direction' consistent. Verbal Positive Approach is physical. Some people initially refer to Verbal Positive Approach as 'positive thinking.' It is different from positive thinking or having a positive attitude. Whatever you think or whatever your attitude, you can still use Verbal Positive Approach. Some people say that a person has to think before speaking. However, there are quite a few people who speak before they think. You may even know a few. I suspect that each of us has developed some speaking habits, thinking habits and attitudinal habits, any of which can occur first, depending on the situation.

Instead of concentrating on niceness, personality or mood, Verbal Positive Approach concentrates on performance and relationships. I've had people tell me that Verbal Positive

Approach helps them to maintain a healthy stress level. I have also had people to tell me that it actually helps them to be nicer.

There have also been many to say that they even get more positive responses from other people when they use Verbal Positive Approach. These skills are designed to provide constant reinforcement for positive direction. When you use these skills, you can continue to approach any situation as you always have. As I said before, keep your savvy; keep your toughness; you can be considerate of others or you can focus only on yourself. Sometimes you may need to be firm; sometimes it is appropriate to be nice or courteous. Of course courtesy is *always* in order. Whatever your feelings, whether you are firm or courteous, you can always use Verbal Positive Approach and still make your point.

Research by Albert Mehrabian and Susan Ferris (1967) shows that 93% of human communication includes 'facial expressions' (55%) and 'tone of voice' (38%). Some have told me that their uses of Verbal Positive Approach influence their body language and speaking tone. That may be true, and it is certainly worth testing. However, this work is designed for you to narrow your concentration to the words that you speak and write. Your '7 percent' may influence everybody else's 93%.

You have learned enough information so far, for us to begin. From now on, we will use the letters OTP to mean 'Other Than Positive' rather than the term 'negative' when referring to certain words. The fundamental skill of Verbal Positive Approach is to take **ALL** of the OTP words out of everything that you say. OTP words are mostly dictionary definitions, such as *don't, won't, can't, wouldn't, couldn't, shouldn't, sad, worry, bad, difficult, not, stupid, ridiculous,* etc.

However much you are accustomed to using these words to express what you have to say, treasures of words are available to you to help you say exactly *what* you want to say, exactly *how* you want to say it in a positive direction.

The language of Consistent Positive Direction includes everyday words like *chair, car, important, do, people, a, and, the,* as well as words like *great, insist, wonderful, must, fantastic,* etc.

**Special case**—When someone asks a question requiring a 'yes' or 'no' answer:

- If the answer is 'Yes,' then say 'Yes.'
- If the answer is 'No' say 'No,' then use Verbal Positive Approach for anything that you say thereafter.

Below are simple, everyday examples of Verbal Positive Approach to show you how easy it can be to use these skills.

**Instead of saying:** Don't forget.
**You can say:** Remember.

**Instead of saying:** I'll never forget you.
**You can say:** I'll always remember you.

**Instead of saying:** If we don't get the order in time, we will not make the shipment.
**You can say:** We need the order in time, to make the shipment.

**Instead of saying:** That is wrong.
**You can say:** That needs to be corrected.
or
Check to see if that is correct.

**Instead of saying:** That is inappropriate behavior.
**You can say:** Use appropriate behavior.

**Instead of saying:** We will not be successful if we don't change the way we communicate.
**You can say:** We need to change the way that we communicate to be successful.
or
Using Consistent Positive Direction increases our chances for success.

**Instead of saying:** This is difficult.
**You can say:** This is going to take some effort.
or
I need to spend some time on this.
or
This will really test your skills.
or
We will have to really concentrate.

**Instead of saying:** You are not strong enough to lift the barrel.
**You Can Say:** You need to be stronger to lift the barrel.
or
Get someone to help you lift the barrel.
**Instead Of Saying:** I don't think they will ever change.
**You can say:** They really need to change.
or
It is important that they change.
or
What will it take for them to change?

**Instead of saying:** You are inconsiderate.
**You can say:** You need to be more considerate.

**Instead of saying:** That is unbelievable!
**You can say:** That is amazing!

**Instead of saying:** We don't have room for any more appointments.
**You can say:** All of our appointments are filled.
or
We need to make room for more appointments.
**Instead of saying:** That is a ridiculous idea.
**You can say:** There must be a better way.
or
How did that idea come up?

**Instead of saying:** That's not a bad idea.
**You can say:** That's a good idea.
or
That's something to consider.

**Instead of saying:** That was very unselfish.
**You can say:** That was very thoughtful.
or
That was very nice [of him/her].

**Instead of saying:** You disappointed me.
**You can say:** I expected more from you.
or
I really depended on you. What happened?
or
I thought you knew how important it was to get this done on time.

Based on these examples and the thousands of sentence-to-sentence opportunities that we have every day to interact with others, it is clear that Verbal Positive Approach provides the core *consistency* in Consistent Positive Direction.

Therefore, it assures consistency in speaking toward the results, the achievements, and the successes that are necessary or desired. Most of the time, your influence can be very simple. When someone says something is "wrong", you can say or ask "What needs to be right?" Many times, those kinds of simple comments can advance the group toward solutions more quickly. Asking, "What needs to be right?" may also help you to get more DO responses.

The skills that you just learned are only the beginning.

## The Numbers

Verbal Positive Approach is the most fundamental skill of Consistent Positive Direction. It feeds every other habit, method and framework of Consistent Positive Direction. You will learn that Verbal Positive Approach is a significant benefit when dealing with the comments of others, as well as your own. If there is an OTP word in your sentence, then change the sentence, or at least recognize the OTP word immediately. Then, think about how you will use Verbal Positive Approach the next time. When you are using or about to use an OTP word, that is the time to change the sentence, be quiet, listen or ask a question. The more you catch yourself, the more the language will become automatic.

Remember this: 1) When you change the sentence, change it so that you still get the point across or so that you speak about future action. 2) Concentrate on changing the sentence, instead of only replacing the OTP word. These skills involve more than just substituting words; David Townsend and Thomas J. Bever (2001) depict the sentence as the fundamental "natural level of linguistic representation." 3) You are using Verbal Positive Approach in your everyday speaking, still being serious or humorous, firm or easy going, emotional or calm and always being yourself. 4) Verbal Positive Approach is a *skill,* rather than how to act.

You are gaining the knowledge to increase your use of the language of Consistent Positive Direction to at least 99.7% of your sentences (based on a 3 sigma performance). The average for most people is 85% or less. This represents a change in the number of sentences with OTP words from 90 per speaking hour (85% Verbal Positive Approach) to 1.8 per speaking hour (99.7%). You actually can measure the use of these skills. This is called your Verbal Positive Fitness.

The following table shows that if the amount of time you speak in a day adds up to 5 hours, prior to learning Verbal Positive Approach, you use an average of 450 OTP words per day, even when you are being positive. You speak in a positive direction in about 85% of your sentences. If you only use Verbal Positive Approach in 80% of your sentences, then the number of OTP words that you use is about 600 per speaking day or 120 per speaking hour.

You are consistent when you use Verbal Positive Approach in over 99.7% of your sentences. You can graduate from using over 450 OTP words per speaking day to using less than 10 per speaking day. As you practice, you will increase your mastery. Once you become consistent, your road to mastery is almost automatic. These skills give you the opportunity to use Consistent Positive Direction *with* your positive attitude.

Now, when you consider (or) think of yourself as a positive person, you can have the language to go with it.

| Verbal Positive Fitness Level | Percentage of Sentences | OTP Words per Speaking Hour |
|---|---|---|
| Average Verbal Positive Fitness | 85% | 90 per speaking hr.<br>(450 per speaking day, based on 5 hrs.) |
| Consistent Verbal Positive Fitness | 99.7% | 1.8 per speaking hr.<br>(9 per speaking day based on 5 hrs.) |
| Mastery Level of Verbal Positive Fitness | 99.9% | 0.6 per speaking hr.<br>(3 per speaking day based on 5 hrs.) |

Verbal Positive Approach also increases the chances of getting positive responses from others. It is suspected that it increases the chances of getting *positive direction* responses from others as well.

Estimating that people speak a little over 600 sentences per hour, your use of Verbal Positive Approach can be very valuable. In a situation where there is a meeting or a discussion, in any given hour, about 600 sentences will be spoken, whether there are 2 people in the room or 100 people in the room. This, of course, assumes that one person is speaking at a time.

Let's say that you have learned Verbal Positive Approach, at least to the point of being consistent (99.7% of your sentences). That means that whenever you talk, you increase the positive direction in the room. If there are others who speak at that level, then there is even more positive direction. So, if you speak 15 minutes of that hour, you know that the group will experience 150 sentences of Verbal Positive Approach. You can possibly influence the positive direction of the meeting. The power is in the *amount* of Verbal Positive Approach that you use.

*You can speak to anybody in a positive direction.* As you learn more and with practice you will be able to make these skills automatic.

## TALKEASE

A friend of mine named Yolanda once shared something with me that one of her college math professors told her. He said, "The more equations that you know, the easier it is to solve the problem." That statement strongly applies to Consistent Positive Direction. You will learn a number of skills that you can use to make it easier to be consistent. TALKEASE involves the use of Verbal Positive Approach in different types of statements that you use in your speaking and writing everyday. They are listed below.

- **Limit Statements** address boundaries.
- **Statements of Emphasis** highlight importance, desire, necessity and intention.
- **Solution-Generating Statements** influence or advance progress.
- **Statements of Preference** express group or individual likes, desires, opinions and needs.
- **Statements of Feelings or Emotion** connect others to your positive direction.
- **Possibility Statements** encourage and talk toward goals and objectives.
- **Assurance Statements** talk toward what needs to happen for successful outcomes.
- **Permission Statements** express rules and 'being allowed.'
- **Conditional Statements** speak about cause and effect.

TALKEASE will help you to make the language of Consistent Positive Direction a habit. The more you practice, the easier it gets. Just as you go to the gym to increase your physical fitness, you practice these skills to increase your Verbal Positive Fitness. For each of the different types of TALKEASE statements, you will be presented with a variety of examples to show you that the language of Consistent Positive Direction can be used in any situation.

**Limit Statements** are used in expressions of time, distance, space, location, actions or boundaries. They are statements that set official boundaries such as "Employees only." They are statements that address narrow options, such as "The best way to develop the new position is to provide adequate training."

Some of the key words for Limit Statements are:

| | |
|---|---|
| **highest/lowest** | **most/least** |
| **better/best** | **earliest/latest** |
| **maximum/minimum** | **top/bottom** |
| **only** | **largest/smallest** |
| **fastest/slowest** | **outside of/inside of** |
| **first/last** | **more than/less than** |

If the word 'not' is a habit of your speaking, the Limit Statements are an excellent way to change the habit. For example: **instead of saying**, "She is not in right now," **you can say**, "The earliest that she will be back is 3:00." **Instead of saying**, "It is not possible to drive to California from New York, in one day," **you can say**, "The fastest that you can drive from New York to California is 2 ½ days." **Instead of saying**, "I have not seen this report before," **you can say**, "This is the first time that I have seen this report."

**Statements of Emphasis** are used to insist, to emphasize feelings, to discipline, to demand, to emphasize ideas, to compliment and more. Just as you can make your point using OTP words, you can effectively make your point using Verbal Positive Approach. You can use words like 'really,' 'certainly,' 'definitely' and other words of emphasis. For example, **instead of saying**, "I do not want you to go outside," **you can say**, "I definitely want you to stay in the house." **Instead of saying**, "You are having dinner with us. I won't take 'no' for an answer". **You can say,** "Of course you are having dinner with us".

Here is a partial list of words and phrases of emphasis:

| | | | |
|---|---|---|---|
| **always** | **amazing** | **best** | **by all means** |
| **certainly** | **definitely** | **especially** | **highest** |
| **important** | **mostly** | **of course** | **only** |
| **please** | **quite** | **really** | **sure** |
| **surprised** | **truly** | **utmost** | **very** |
| **well** | | | |

Perhaps you can think of others. There are many.

**Skill Exercise:** Change the sentences below into the language of Consistent Positive Direction and include a word of emphasis in each of your changes. For example: **instead of saying**, "Don't forget to follow the instructions," **you can say**, "It is very important that you remember to follow the instructions."

Change these sentences before you continue. Use emphasis.

1. I've never seen anything like that before.

______________________________________________

______________________________________________

______________________________________________

______________________________________________

2. I don't like the way that you talk to me.

______________________________________________

______________________________________________

______________________________________________

______________________________________________

3. That is not the right way to do it.

______________________________________________

______________________________________________

______________________________________________

______________________________________________

**Here are possible changes to the sentences above. The changes that you made are probably as good or better.**

1) This is the very first time that I've seen anything like that.
2) Please speak to me with respect from now on.
3) There's definitely a better way to do it!

Take a few minutes to think of other positive direction changes to the same sentences.

Many people think that the OTP word emphasizes the point. However, in our everyday speaking the body language and tone of voice make the point. Instead of saying, "I will NOT go without you!" you can be just as firm by saying, "I will ONLY go if you go." You can always make your point using Consistent Positive Direction. If you feel that what you say is too weak, *insist* on it in a positive direction. Let someone know that you *absolutely* mean what you say!

**Solution Generating Statements** appear in many forms. The real power is to speak in such a way that you influence forward movement. Use Solution Generating Statements to influence creativity, to stimulate thinking, and to help develop opportunities. Use Solution Generating Statements to sustain confidence in your leadership, to bolster diplomacy, political campaigns and alliances.

The best Solution Generating Statements are questions. First, we will address some habits that many of us have developed in our lives.

We commonly use phrases like:
"Isn't that…?"
"Don't you…?"
"Why don't…?"
"Aren't we…?"

**Instead of saying**, "Isn't that what I told you?" **you can say**, "That is what I told you; right?"

**Instead of saying**, "Don't you have some experience in running that machine?" **you can say**, "Is it true that you have some experience in running that machine?"

**Instead of saying**, "Why don't we consider asking each other a few questions?" **you can say**, "Suppose we consider asking each other a few questions?"

**Instead of saying**, "Aren't you going to the store?" **you can say**, "You are going to the store; right?"

Solution Generating Statements can talk about improvements or corrections needed, rather than saying something is "wrong." Yes, 'wrong' is an OTP word. So, **instead of saying**, "You are using the wrong process," **you can say**, "You need to use the correct process..." or "Before you go any further, switch to the correct process." **Instead of saying**, "The disrespect, on the job has got to stop," **you can say**, "We have to be more respectful of each other on the job."

Rather than using the word 'problem,' find other ways to express the need for changes to be made. When we use the word 'problem,' we are most often talking about something that we want to get 'away from.' We always have the opportunity to talk about what we want to 'move toward.' **Instead of saying**, "We have a problem with that," **you can say**, "I think we need to approach that differently" or "How can we all be more comfortable with that decision?"

Solution Generating Statements open the way for new or improved ideas. **Instead of saying**, "We are not going to get anywhere if we don't work together," **you can say**, "We can make significant progress if we work together."

If you are involved and you want progress, put Consistent Positive Direction at the center, even if you are the only person in the room who knows the skills.

**Skill Exercise**—Change these sentences before you continue. Use Solution Generating Statements.

1. Why can't we work together?

________________________________________________

________________________________________________

________________________________________________

________________________________________________

2. We are not safe in our neighborhood.

________________________________________________________

________________________________________________________

________________________________________________________

________________________________________________________

3. Don't leave your room in such a mess.

________________________________________________________

________________________________________________________

________________________________________________________

________________________________________________________

**Here are possible changes to the sentences. The changes that you made are probably as good or better.**

1) Let's improve the way that we work together.
2) What will make our neighborhood safer?
3) Make sure your room is neat before you leave.
Take a few minutes to think of other positive direction changes to the same sentences.

**Statements of Preference** are your way to express your preferences, in the language of Consistent Positive Direction. Some key words to express preference are: better, rather, want, like, prefer or wish.

**Skill Exercise**—Change these sentences before you continue. Use Statements of Preference:

1. I don't like your sneakers.

________________________________________________________

________________________________________________________

________________________________________________________

________________________________________________________

2. You shouldn't lean back in your chair.

______________________________________________

______________________________________________

______________________________________________

______________________________________________

3. You can't do it that way.

______________________________________________

______________________________________________

______________________________________________

______________________________________________

4. Never do a job half way.

______________________________________________

______________________________________________

______________________________________________

______________________________________________

5. Nobody talks like that to me.

______________________________________________

______________________________________________

______________________________________________

______________________________________________

6. I will not share my office with another person.

______________________________________________

______________________________________________

______________________________________________

______________________________________________

7. Why don't you keep your room clean?

____________________________________________

____________________________________________

____________________________________________

____________________________________________

**Here are possible changes to the sentences. The changes that you made are probably as good or better.**

1) I think you would look much better in another pair of sneakers.
2) I would rather you sit up straight in your chair.
3) I want you to do it correctly.
4) I always like a job done correctly.
5) I prefer that you talk to me with respect.
6) I want an office to myself.
7) I wish you would keep your room clean!

Take a few minutes to think of other positive direction changes to the same sentences.

**Statements of Feeling or Emotion** help you to focus yourself and others forward. Our feelings are impacted by many circumstances and it takes some effort, at times, to speak in a positive direction. Your desires, your expectations, your opportunities all require emotional energy. How do you consistently express that energy in a positive direction, even when the most compelling demands impact your life? When your Consistent Positive Direction becomes an automatic skill, you will be able to express yourself with the same intensity. Sometimes people think that they have to take away their emotions to use these skills. Remember, you can use Consistent Positive Direction and still be yourself.

**Skill Exercise**—Change these sentences before you continue. Use Statements of Feeling or Emotion.

1. I was very disappointed that I missed the trip last week.

____________________________________________________________
____________________________________________________________
____________________________________________________________
____________________________________________________________

2. I am angry with you for being late!

____________________________________________________________
____________________________________________________________
____________________________________________________________
____________________________________________________________

3. I don't want to talk to you right now.

____________________________________________________________
____________________________________________________________
____________________________________________________________
____________________________________________________________

**Here are possible changes to the sentences. The changes that you made are probably as good or better.**

1) I really wanted to go on that trip, last week.
2) I expected you to be on time. You knew how important this was to me!
3) It is best that I talk to you after I calm down.

Take a few minutes to think of other positive direction changes to the same sentences.

**Possibility Statements** talk about what can or needs to be accomplished. If you want success, talk success; if you want peace, talk peace; if you want trust, talk trust. Possibility Statements have power. We influence others to create possibilities. We influence ourselves to create possibilities. Others can also influence us. The possibilities that we create can come from anywhere. They can occur at anytime. They can be triggered by anyone. Moreover, you have the choice about how much you want to turn a possibility into a reality. Your ideas, your dreams and your realities are the fuel that feed the future. They come from anywhere and they can go anywhere. You have the awesome power to express them in a positive direction.

One evening in the early '90's, I was driving on Interstate 95, headed north toward Delaware. I was listening to National Public Radio. Vice President Al Gore was speaking to the National Press Club. His topic was the "Information Super Highway." As I was listening, a major brainstorm was brewing. I started thinking that Verbal Positive Approach could easily be used for e-mail and other documents and texts transmitted via the information super highway. That led me to think that a computer program could be developed so that people could readily do Verbal Positive Approach checks on their computer documents, texts and e-mails in ways similar to 'spell checks.' At that point, my idea was a possibility. Today it is a reality. With the technical creativity and programming expertise of Phil Ebling, a Verbal Positive Approach check was designed for Windows. It can be called up as readily as a 'spell check.' Phil created the software; I designed the approach and parameters.

Talk possibilities rather than limitations. **Instead of saying**, "It is very difficult to run in the sand," **you can say**, "It takes a lot of effort to run in the sand." **Instead of saying**, "It is hard to study at night," **you can say**, "I have to find a way to make it easier to study at night."

**Skill Exercise**—Change these sentences before you continue. Use Possibility Statements.

1. We cannot be successful if we are not careful.

________________________________________________

________________________________________________

________________________________________________

________________________________________________

2. It is impossible for them to be fair.

________________________________________________

________________________________________________

________________________________________________

________________________________________________

3. You will have a difficult time getting an 'A.'

________________________________________________

________________________________________________

________________________________________________

________________________________________________

**Here are possible changes to the sentences. The changes that you made are probably as good or better.**

1) To be successful, we have to be careful.
2) It is essential that they learn fairness.
3) Use the time and effort necessary to get an 'A.'

Take a few minutes to think of other positive direction changes to the same sentences.

**Assurance Statements** talk toward what needs to happen. For example, **instead of saying**, "Don't let anyone stop you," **you**

**can say**, "Do what it takes to keep moving forward." **Instead of saying**, "Don't lose," **you can say**, "Win." **Instead of saying**, "Don't fall," **you can say**, "Be careful." **Instead of saying**, "Don't fail," **you can say**, "Succeed."

Many times we speak of prevention: preventing accidents, preventing violence, preventing failure, preventing defects, preventing poverty. 'Prevention' speaks of what we want to 'get away from…' 'Assurance' speaks of what we want to 'move toward.' **Instead of saying**, "Prevent mistakes," **you can say**, "Assure correctness."

**Skill Exercise**—Change the following phrases before you continue; use Assurance Statements.

1. Prevent failure…

______________________________________________

______________________________________________

______________________________________________

______________________________________________

2. Prevent defects…

______________________________________________

______________________________________________

______________________________________________

______________________________________________

3. Prevent violence…

______________________________________________

______________________________________________

______________________________________________

______________________________________________

4. Prevent poverty…

____________________________________________________

____________________________________________________

____________________________________________________

____________________________________________________

**Here are possible changes to the phrases. The changes that you made are probably as good or better.**

1) Assure success…
2) Assure accuracy…
3) Assure peace…
4) Assure prosperity…

Take a few minutes to think of other positive direction changes to the same phrases.

**Permission Statements** are statements that are used for controlling and directing actions and activities. Permission Statements are expressed as rules, as 'being allowed' or as conditional statements. **Instead of saying**, "You are not allowed to run in the sand," **you can say**, "You are only allowed to run on the grass or the sidewalk." **Instead of saying**, "You cannot watch television if you do not do your homework," **you can say**, "You can watch television after you do your homework."

**Skill Exercise**—Change these sentences before you continue. Use Permission Statements.

1. Rules: Requests cannot be handed in after Tuesday.

____________________________________________________

____________________________________________________

____________________________________________________

____________________________________________________

2. Being allowed: You are not allowed to go to Jerome's house, today.

____________________________________________

____________________________________________

____________________________________________

____________________________________________

3. Conditional Statement: If you do not do the dishes, you can't go to the movies.

____________________________________________

____________________________________________

____________________________________________

____________________________________________

**Here are possible changes to the sentences. The changes that you made are probably as good or better.**

1) Requests must be handed in by Tuesday.
2) You have to stay home today.
3) You have to do the dishes before you go to the movies.

Take a few minutes to think of other positive direction changes to the same sentences.

**Conditional Statements** speak loosely or empirically about cause and effect. Many conditional statements include the words 'if' and 'then.' For example, "If you use that light, then the room will be brighter," or "If you go to the store today, then you can save 10% on your grocery bill." They most often express that, if or when something occurs, something will result from that occurrence. Some Permission Statements are also Conditional Statements (see Permission Statements).

**Skill Exercise**—Change the following phrases before you continue; use Conditional Statements.

1. If you keep running away from it, you will not learn how to be comfortable around it.

____________________________________________________________
____________________________________________________________
____________________________________________________________
____________________________________________________________

2. If you keep talking like that, you will never be successful.

____________________________________________________________
____________________________________________________________
____________________________________________________________
____________________________________________________________

3. Whenever you go out on the weekend, you don’t get enough work done.

____________________________________________________________
____________________________________________________________
____________________________________________________________
____________________________________________________________

4. I can’t run this machine correctly if you keep me in meetings all day.

____________________________________________________________
____________________________________________________________
____________________________________________________________
____________________________________________________________

**Here are possible changes to the phrases. The changes that you made are probably as good or better.**

1) If you stay around it long enough, you will learn to be more comfortable around it.
2) If you want success, talk success.
3) It may be important to arrange your weekend schedules so that you can do all of your work.
4) It is best to schedule meetings so that I have adequate time to run this machine correctly.

Take a few minutes to think of other positive direction changes to the same sentences.

**Do you have to know the difference?**

At any given time, you may say that a Solution Generating Statement is a Possibility Statement, or a Statement of Feeling or Emotion is a Statement of Preference. Any interpretation that you make is okay. They can overlap. The purpose of the TALKEASE section of this book is to express some of the many ways that you can use the language of Consistent Positive Direction. There are more.

Some say that it takes a lot of concentration to use Verbal Positive Approach. Initially, it does require concentration. However, the more you use it, the more it becomes automatic. It's like driving. Two important physical aspects of driving are *steering* and *using the brakes*. Those who drive know that steering and using the brakes become automatic. People learn how to drive and then they learn how to do it well. Every time they drive they get more practice.

Just as steering and using the brakes become automatic to the driver, Verbal Positive Approach becomes automatic in speaking and writing. Driving is a physical skill. The language of Consistent Positive Direction is a physical skill. The simplicity of Consistent Positive Direction is to use Verbal Positive Approach in over 99.7% of your sentences, in any situation, under any circumstances. As you learn more techniques and approaches, Verbal Positive Approach continues to be the core of your consistency. Providing names for different approaches helps to give you a deeper understanding of the language of Consistent Positive Direction. Yet, instead of trying to memorize the names of so many skills, just understand and use the guidelines of Verbal Positive Approach (see Guidelines following). Instead of being selective about when you use the language of Consistent Positive Direction, use it all of the time. The more you use the skills of Consistent Positive Direction, the more you are likely to use them *when what you have to say really matters*.

## Silent Practice

The most powerful skill of Consistent Positive Direction is 'Silent Practice.' Very simply, instead of telling someone that you are using Consistent Positive Direction, *just use it*. Those who know the skills use Silent Practice both in everyday speaking and in high powered interactions. People notice something different about them. For me, people often make comments about the interesting points that I make and how my comments give them an added perspective. I say "thank you," knowing that using these skills helped me to influence more positive direction and positive direction results among the people with whom I interact.

The reason to use Silent Practice is that, if you tell people that you use Consistent Positive Direction, they might spend valuable time and energy saying that you are using some of that 'positive stuff' on them. Silent Practice keeps the movement forward. Yet, if people are curious enough to ask about what you are doing, or how you are communicating so effectively, it is perfectly all right to tell them. If it were a secret, then it would be called Secret Practice.

## Guidelines

Here are the guidelines and key ingredients for becoming very good at using the language of Consistent Positive Direction:

**Consistent Positive Direction Guidelines**

- **You want to do it.**
- **Be yourself.** Use it in real life, in every conversation. It is a real life skill.
- **Use it all the time.** Make yourself use the language of Consistent Positive Direction under any circumstances; it will grow to become second nature.
- **Catch yourself**, as you are using or about to use an OTP word. Correcting yourself is as simple as knowing what to say next time.
    - If the word is about to come out, then change the sentence, be quiet, listen or ask a question.
    - If the word has already come out, then figure out how to say the sentence, the next time.
    - Be nice to yourself; be patient with yourself.
- **Give others their space.** If there are others who are learning the skills, be mindful that they may want to learn at their own pace. Help one another if everyone agrees.

Whatever your attitude, whatever your thinking, you can always use the language of Consistent Positive Direction effectively. When you are at a standstill, the language of

Consistent Positive Direction will guide you, even if it is only to ask a question.

I previously worked for a major corporation. At one point, my job title was International Sales Coordinator (ISC). During that time I was already practicing the language of Consistent Positive Direction quite well. One day I was given a project to find ways to increase our performance in 'on time' deliveries—getting the product to the customer on time more often. Our current 'on time' delivery rate was close to 89%. I called a meeting of my manager and some key people on our Customer Service team to explain the issue and to get clear about what had to be done. I thought the meeting went well and that we would make a good start.

One of my ISC counterparts attended the meeting. I stopped by his office to get his thoughts about the meeting. He said very bluntly, yet respectfully, "The meeting wasn't worth a [#!%*]…" Of course, I wanted to hear a different response. I wanted him to say that the meeting was great and that it was about time we worked on the issue. After a quiet jolt on my feelings, I wanted to defend the way I handled the meeting. In situations like that, it is easy to use OTP words to respond to such a comment, perhaps saying something like "You didn't understand what I was trying to do…" At times like that, I am grateful that Consistent Positive Direction is automatic for me. I was wondering what to say. Of course I would use the language of Consistent Positive Direction. That was one time that I consciously thought that the best skill to use, was to ask a question (getting answers to questions helps you to know what to say next). After standing there a few seconds, I asked, "What do you mean?" He said to me, "You didn't have the right people there. They didn't care about or understand most of what you were trying to do." I said, "Who should have been there?" He said, "I don't know but you didn't have anybody from the plant in that meeting." It was best for me to ask questions.

Moreover, rather than react to his comments, I allowed the language of Consistent Positive Direction to carry me through the conversation, even if it was only to ask questions. I said, "Who are the right people?

What suggestions do you have?" It turned out that my questions caused him to give me the answers that I needed, in a positive direction. As he was talking, I realized that he was right, although I wanted to be right. I started to think about the people that needed to be a part of making this effort successful, people that I may only talk to once a month instead of every day. We were at headquarters. We saw the *numbers*, but the *action* was at the manufacturing plant, a few hundred miles away. The products were sent hundreds, even thousands of miles, daily, from the plant to customers everywhere. The inventory was also held at the plant. I needed to get the folks at the plant involved.

So after I figured out the right people for the project, I arranged a conference call which included the people at the plant. The outcome of that conference call alone was an increase to 94% consistent 'on time' performance, within 2 weeks. Meanwhile, we started a small team to work on the issue in more detail. Within 2 months, our 'on time' performance was close to 97%.

My use of Consistent Positive Direction helped me through that initial conversation. Even with the comments of my counterpart, the comments and questions that I used brought out his knowledge and suggestions in a positive direction.

You can do the same thing and you can do it often, with successful results. Just use **AC** Power (The AC stands for **A**t the **C**enter). Put yourself **A**t the **C**enter to influence the change that needs to take place. You will sometimes be the only person in the room that knows how to use Consistent Positive Direction. However, remember under those circumstances your use of the skills outnumbers everyone else's.

Reminder: Consistent Positive Direction is a **skill** to speak in a positive direction rather than to *be* positive. Positive Direction is the direction of the required and desired results, accomplishments, achievements, goals, objectives and/or successes. It can be a full glass or an empty glass, forward or reverse, up or down, one side or the other.

Here is an example. You can be positive by saying, “I am so proud of you; you didn’t forget your books, today.” Using the language of Consistent Positive Direction, you can say, “I am so proud of you; you *remembered* your books, today.” The required result was to remember the books.

Now, take a break. Go and practice your new skills. If you play a sport or an instrument, there are only certain times and places that you can practice that sport or that instrument. However, you can practice the language of Consistent Positive Direction all of the time and everywhere, every time you speak. The more you practice, the faster it will become automatic.

You can take charge of *your* positive direction. When you come back, you will learn how to apply the skills to your attitude.

# Chapter 3

## ABOVE THE CLOUDS: The Positive Directions of Your Attitude

If you truly made an effort to use your new found skills, you probably experienced hesitation in the middle of a number of your spoken sentences. It seems to be easier to write using Verbal Positive Approach than it is to speak using Verbal Positive Approach. You probably found that you use more OTP words than you thought. These are the same normal experiences that you have when you are learning to drive a car, learning to play a sport, a musical instrument or even learning to play a video game. The skills require practice.

As you practice more, you will be more fluent in your use of the language of Consistent Positive Direction. It will be as easy, or easier to use the language in speaking as it is in writing. Once you reach the use of the language in 99.7% of your sentences, you will get even better. It will become as automatic as your use of the rest of the English language. So, continue to practice. Whenever you leave this book, you can practice the skills every time you speak or write. Just like driving or any other skill, the *more* you do it, the *better* you do it. You learn the skills by 'doing.'

At this point, you may still feel that you must approach situations or circumstances with a positive attitude. You may even still think that a positive attitude is what Consistent Positive Direction is all about. *Remember, whatever your attitude, you can still use the language of* Consistent Positive Direction.

In this chapter you will learn how to *attitudinize yourself in a positive direction*, in any situation, under any circumstances. This is the core ability that helps you to use Consistent Positive Direction on the inside as well as interacting with others on the outside. It is important that you understand to use the complete phrase *attitudinize yourself or myself in a positive direction,* because attitudes can be expressed either way.

Attitudes exist everywhere: in the home, in the workplace, in stores, in the classroom, in gatherings, in our own perceptions of other human beings, in groups, small and large. Anywhere you go there are as many attitudes as there are people, including your own.

There are two positive direction abilities that will help you to attitudinize yourself in a positive direction: Exercise Complete Respect in a Positive Direction and Practice **T**otal **O**pen **L**istening and **L**earning (**TOLL**) in a Positive Direction.

## Exercise Complete Respect in a Positive Direction

Respect is the core of relationships and relationships are what make today's families, businesses and organizations work. When respect is exercised in a positive direction, it adds *power* to relationships. Additionally, when respect is exercised to treat others the way *they* want to be treated, it adds *value and meaning* to relationships. Here are examples of respect in a positive direction.

Oftentimes, we hear phrases like "I don't want to hurt their feelings" or "I don't want them to think or feel… etc." Just as easily, a person can say, "I want them to feel comfortable" or "I want them to feel supported by our efforts." Very simply, talk toward the results that you want. In this case, the desired result was to want the person to feel comfortable or wanting other people to feel supported. If we learn that a person wants to be heard more or wants to be valued, then find ways to listen more. Find ways for the person to know that you *do* value her input. Sometimes people just have to know. Sometimes it is as easy as telling them.

In a conversation about respect in the workplace one day, a colleague, Nick Cirilli asked a very simple question. "Where is the line? How far do I go with my comments toward or about someone else?" Many times when we have strong differences of beliefs or opinions with people or we want to make people pay for what they did, we feel that we have a 'perfectly good right' to say anything that we want to them, *and/or* about them. We even go as far as getting other people and friends on our side. Sometimes those feelings are so strong, that it would probably take more than anything that I could tell you for you to be respectful anyway.

I have often been in situations in which I wanted to make someone pay for what they did so much that I felt perfectly justified to say anything that I wanted to them and do everything that I could to get others to feel the same way. However, as I learned more about respect, I realized how much I could be in control of what comes out of my mouth. I would love to say that I am the perfect example of how to respect everyone. Truthfully? I have to work at it and there are times when it requires more effort than others. I *can* say that I have improved significantly. I do know that when I get to the name calling or language that could take away the esteem of another person, I've gone over the line. I call it the "Cirilli Line". I am also learning to help people to PLAY rather than making them pay – educating someone on how to be more respectful in a way that we can work together more productively.

True expressions of Complete Respect include respecting others when they are out of our sight, the same way as if they are in our presence. If you want to talk about someone or a group, make sure it is okay to talk about them or to poke fun or to call them names that could take away from their self-esteem. If you question whether it would be okay to talk about them that way, it is best to be quiet. Of course, you can take a minute to go and ask. Most important, rather than putting conditions on whether you will respect others, respect others anyway, whether they are in the room or out of the room.

Complete Respect includes two other considerations: 1) the Golden Rule: "Do unto others as you would have them do unto you." In other words, treat others the way that you would like to be treated. Whenever you have strong differences of opinions or beliefs, you can use the Golden Rule. 2) The Platinum Rule, according to Dr. Tony Alessandra and Dr. Michael J. O'Connor (1998): "Do unto others as *they'd* like done unto them." Sometimes people just want their names spelled correctly or they just want a 'fair chance' or they want to be valued customers. Treating others the way that they want to be treated is the expression of your respect for the value and needs of others in your daily interactions.

**Complete Respect includes your use of four abilities:**

- **Respect everyone anyway**
- **Respect everyone whether they are in the room or out of the room**
- **Treat others the way *you* would want to be treated**
- **Treat others the way that *they* would want to be treated**

These are called abilities because you can control what comes out of your mouth *and* you can express those abilities in a positive direction.

It would be great if we could be respectful of everyone in exactly the same way. However, the people of the world are born, raised and live in different cultures. There are many different ways of life. Different things are important to different people. Even as you possess those four powerful abilities to exercise Complete Respect, you need different approaches. The many ways to approach the differences that exist among us are characterized by five (5) domains.

The Five Domains of Complete Respect include:

- **Cultural Respect**
- **Social Respect**
- **Professional Respect**
- **Temporal Respect**
- **Spatial Respect**

The more you master these domains, the more power you will add to relationships. That power translates into moving things forward, getting things done and realizing successes. Differences often impact our attitudes.

As we examine each domain of Complete Respect, we will see the many ways in which we identify the *differentness* among us. I use the term *differentness* to acknowledge that we possess uniqueness as well as differences. To me, the term *differences* may only speak of what is different among us, at the *expense* of what is unique in each of us. The domains of Complete Respect help us to understand and adjust to the differentness of others. Knowing more about how to exercise Complete Respect, makes it easier to attitudinize yourself in a positive direction.

**Cultural Respect** is respecting others for who they are anyway—their physical nature, their beliefs and their ethnicity. Treat cultural differentness with Complete Respect. Each of us belongs to a number of identity groups that contribute to who and what we are—our cultural identity. On any given day, more than ever in history, each of us has the opportunity to be around someone who has a different cultural identity. In the United States, because of events of the past, laws, regulations and executive orders were created to protect the civil rights of particular groups including: race, religion, color, sex, national origin, age, physical ability, status as a parent and most recently sexual orientation.

The Civil Rights Act of 1964, the Americans with Disabilities Act of 1990, Executive Order 11246, and the establishment of the Equal Employment Opportunity Commission are cornerstone examples of protecting us for who we are. Of course, there are other groups including families, schools, communities where we are raised and many others that helped to shape our culture. At the same time, they contribute to our own uniqueness. My parents, my place of birth, the elementary school that I attended, the communities where I was raised, getting older and the color of my skin occurred outside of my control. Yet, there could be circumstances that we choose at some points in our lives that could also have a cultural impact that lasts. For example, indoctrination and life in the military has changed the way I walk; also, I noticed a few short years ago that at the end of a meal, I place my utensils on my plate the same way that I did 30 years ago, as a midshipman at the U.S. Naval Academy.

Exercising Cultural Respect everyday helps to create a higher regard and respect toward people with inherent differences; thus, reducing the frequency of enforcement. Therefore, treat cultural differentness with Complete Respect.

**Social Respect** is respecting others in relation to their preferences, customs or habits. Treat social differentness with Complete Respect.

Exercising Social Respect means to respect others in the ways that they *do* things differently. For example, because you are a meat eater, does that mean that you should eat at a separate table from the vegetarians? No! It means that you can invite the vegetarians to eat at your table and you can have vegetarian meals for them. You can accommodate their differentness.

We have many different preferences: the clothes we wear, the ice cream we like, the vehicles we drive and the vehicles we want. We have many different customs: the way we eat, some folks like oceans, some like mountains and some like city streets. With the mobility that we experience in this country, we can easily witness and be a part of a higher volume of preferences, customs and habits, in one place, more than ever in history. Some of those preferences, customs and habits reside inside of us at work. They also help to identify our individuality and similarities. Remember. Treat social differentness with Complete Respect.

**Professional Respect** is respecting others, whoever they are, especially in your decision-making. Treat professional differentness with Complete Respect.

Professional Respect focuses on the respect that you have for others in the workplace, in matters of performance, opportunity, advancement and status. Cultural Respect and Social Respect are respecting a person for who he/she is individually. Exercising Professional Respect means that if two or more people perform the same task or have the same rank, they have an equitable chance for opportunities or advancement whoever they are as individuals.

There are many reasons why we bypass others. However, if it is because of cultural or social differentness, it is affecting business and professional judgment. So, Professional Respect is essential to learning, morale, productivity, bottom line performance and otherwise good business and professional judgment. Additionally, input or contributions can come in different styles from different people. It is important to recognize and accept that individuals do different things in different ways. In his book *Adaptors and Innovators*, Michael Kirton (1989) shows that even though we all have different styles, we all are capable of creativity. Professional respect allows that to happen. So, treat professional differentness with Complete Respect.

**Temporal Respect** is respecting the balance of time and effort that is important to others. Treat temporal differentness with Complete Respect.

Balancing time and effort, means balancing what is important. So, as important as time is to each of our lives, what we do with that time is what matters. That is why we say that Temporal Respect is respect for the 'balance of time' that is important to someone. Take a few minutes to think about what is important to you and how it needs to be respected. What is the best way that the things that are important to you can be honored? Take another few minutes to think about whether you know, respect or have even asked what is important to others with whom you interact in your personal or professional life. What is the best way that you can honor the things that are important to them?

Understandably, something that is important to you may be less important to someone else and something that is important to someone with whom you interact may be less important to you. For example, at the end of each work day, a person *has to* leave at exactly 4:30 for personal reasons. Her co-workers often spend about ten minutes talking about the day and even talking about her, since she has to leave everyday at that time. In this case, her co-workers could exercise Temporal Respect, by understanding and honoring what is important to her by making sure that they share any key information with her that was discussed after hours.

In the workplace, the job must get done. Therefore we may have to make decisions sometimes that may override circumstances or situations that are important to others. When such firmness is required, it can still be executed with respect. Those are times when we exercise the four abilities of complete respect that were shared earlier. Even when I must say "No" or "Do it" or take disciplinary action, I can:

- Respect everyone anyway
- Respect everyone whether they are in the room or out of the room
- Treat others the way I would want to be treated
- Treat others the way that *they* would want to be treated

Those abilities are always available and they also help you to take that extra ounce of time to say and do the right thing. These considerations are especially important if you are in a leadership position.

There are also things that are important to us that require zero time, yet still require respect. The simplest example is making sure that you pronounce and spell names correctly. Our names are important to us. Respect how people want to be addressed. That is an example of "Treating people the way that *they* want to be treated".

You have tremendous opportunities to express respect for the balance of time and/or effort that is important to others, in ways that build relationships. Importantly, rather than trying to figure out someone's Temporal Domain, just understand that he or she has one. Therefore, treat temporal differentness with Complete Respect.

**Spatial Respect** is respecting the self-esteem, responsibility and personal space of others. Treat spatial differentness with Complete Respect.

Spatial means pertaining to space. An open field is space. There is space in your house. There is a certain amount of working space that you have on the job, whether it is an office, a machine, or a vehicle. It is important to respect the space of others, even if it is borrowed, rented or assigned. Let's call that kind of space 'physical space.'

Another type of space is an invisible space. Everyone likes to know that he/she has some power, some status, some importance. Let's call this space *empowered* space. It is the freedom that a person has to function, operate, or make decisions. On the job, this freedom ranges from being limited to very specific tasks, to making decisions for an entire organization. Whatever empowered space a person has, Spatial Respect says to support that empowerment in a way that each individual is appreciated, even celebrated for what he/she contributes to the effort. Just as everyone functions in physical space, everyone also functions in empowered space. When you work with others, help each other to be successful. Respect the responsibilities that others have as well as your own.

In many of the workshops and seminars that I have conducted for organizations, I often asked participants, "How do you want to be treated in the workplace?" Among the many answers, the overwhelming response is "…with respect… " How much does the respect that others express toward you impact your effort on the job or at home? How much does the respect that you express toward others impact their efforts on the job or in school? Respect is connected to everything. Treat spatial differentness with Complete Respect.

## Practice Total Open Listening and Learning (TOLLing)

**TOLL** is an acronym for **T**otal **O**pen **L**istening and **L**earning. We are and were often told to listen: by our parents, by our teachers, by our friends, by our managers and supervisors, by our spouses and even by ourselves. During your years in school and beyond, if you had a listening class of any type, you are very fortunate. Most of us had to 'play it by ear,' literally. Yet listening, being as much a part of the language of human communication as speaking and writing, helps us to gain, process and translate information that impacts our everyday realities.

Consider these next few paragraphs as a class in listening. More importantly, you will learn more about what you can do with your listening. Let's start by understanding that speech speed in human communication is about 125-200 words per minute. Thought speed is about 600-800 words per minute. So, we think about four times faster than we speak. That could give us plenty of down time in our thinking and listening, or it could give us plenty of process time. Using that process time well is an awesome power.

There are four major elements of TOLLing:

- Open Listening
- Total Self Listening
- 7th Sense Listening
- 7th Sense Learning

When referring to *openness* in Consistent Positive Direction, it means to be open to what comes in. Be open to receiving information, observations and experiences. Then you have a more clear opportunity to translate your high-speed thoughts into a positive direction.

**Open Listening** means to take in information before you process or judge the information, and before you speak. When you are listening to someone with *your* reality, you are probably listening with filters, sometimes translating the information into what you think you hear. As you listen, the best way to be more correct about the reality of someone else is to set your reality aside. Be open to the information that comes in. Then manage what comes out of your mouth.

**Total Self Listening** means to listen with all of your senses: sight, touch, hearing, smell and taste. It is easy to understand that we listen with our ears. Yet we are listening with our eyes, skin, nose and mouth as we experience our 5 senses. The coordinator of the listening effort is the mind, where information is gathered, learned and analyzed. In his book *The Art of Peace,* Morihei Ueshiba (2002), refers to six senses (eyes, ears, nose, tongue, body and mind). The mind is your management tool, the sixth sense. The more it is open to freely accepting information in different ways, the better equipped it is to send the correct information out. First, translate in a positive direction; then speak. When we read the newspaper we are listening with our eyes. When we feel temperature or touch something, we are listening with our body. We gather information using our physical senses, whether through smelling the air or tasting our food. Many of us have been taught to listen to be polite. The true benefit of listening is the gathering of information. That way we can make better decisions. It may take effort to identify the moods and attitudes of others from the information that we receive. However, we have the ability to identify direction.

**7th Sense Listening** is the ability to readily recognize the direction in which someone communicates whether it is positive direction or otherwise. You may often listen to others speak or write using quite a few OTP words. The chances are high that you may be the only person in a group that knows and understands Consistent Positive Direction. This sensitivity is a *trigger to act*. You can choose to speak or write in response, you can wait to receive more information, or you can let it go. It really is your choice.

If you choose to act, here are some example comments and Consistent Positive Direction responses.

**Comment:** I don't think we will ever see any progress with our effort.
**Your Response:** What needs to be done to make progress?
**Comment:** You can't do it that way and expect it to be OK.
**Your Response:** What is the best way to do it?
**Comment:** They didn't give us the directions. How do they expect us to do this?
**Your Response:** Looks like we better get the directions. What is the telephone number?

Your 7th Sense Listening is your positive direction compass. It tells you the direction of statements, situations and circumstances that are used by yourself and others. Whenever you choose to speak or write, you will have opportunities to re-channel, redirect or refocus the direction. Of course, some situations require more effort and patience than others and you may have to use more than a few comments. You will be able to interact, using Consistent Positive Direction, whatever time or effort is required.

**7th Sense Learning** is your ability to translate what you experience into Consistent Positive Direction or to readily identify positive direction. This is an ability that can be used often and immediately. It is important to note that expressing your learning in a positive direction is different from being extra nice, extra polite or particularly accommodating. You can always be as direct as you want and/or as polite as you want and you can always express your point.

Here are some examples:

1) "Since my stay in the town of Decker, I know that I will never live where it gets that cold."
**Can be changed to:**
"Since experiencing the cold weather in the town of Decker, I will only live where it is warm."

2) "Based on my experiences with Arthur, I don't think you should approach him about your idea."
**Can be changed to:**
"Based on my experience with Arthur, it is much better for you to approach someone else about your idea."

3) "It sounds like you are not in favor of the idea."
**Can be changed to:**
"It sounds like you want to hear another idea."

Expressing your learnings in a positive direction is also one of the best thinking tools that you can use, whether you say it out loud or keep it to yourself. It helps you to keep your realities in a positive direction. It helps you to always stay focused forward and to more easily work the thoughts, ideas and realities of others into a positive direction.

Remember, practicing **T**otal **O**pen **L**istening and **L**earning in a positive direction means to:

- Be open to what comes in.
- Listen with all of your senses.
- Hear direction.
- Translate your listening and learning into the language of Consistent Positive Direction before you speak.

**T**otal **O**pen **L**istening and **L**earning is also essential to consistently exercising the skills of Complete Respect. Everyday, we have opportunities to listen with our five physical senses and to discern with our minds. Listening and learning is respectful. If you have occasion to ask someone about himself or herself, or about an idea or opinion, listening to the response is a respectful courtesy, as well as a possible learning experience. At one point in her life, whenever my daughter would express her concerns or the particular demands on her life, I would be very quick to provide fatherly advice. One day she said to me, "Dad, sometimes when I tell you what is happening with me, I just want you to listen." She was 17 at the time. That was a turning point in our relationship and it gave me a broader understanding of what it means to respect others. Since then, whenever she started to involve me in a serious conversation, I have asked her, "Do you want my thoughts and suggestions or do you want me to just listen?"

When you consistently include listening as an element of respect as well as a tool for learning, you will cultivate stronger relationships, even with yourself. Listening is also fundamental to *attitudinizing yourself in a positive direction.*

## Attitudinize Yourself in a Positive Direction

Attitudinize yourself in a positive direction by first listening to yourself. Whenever thoughts or ideas come to you, allow yourself to take them in, with the same thoughtfulness that you use to listen to others. As you learn these skills of Consistent Positive Direction, it becomes easier to hear and to feel the direction of your thoughts. Consequently, it is easier to translate them into a positive direction. When you attitudinize yourself in a positive direction, you are positioned to exercise complete respect for your own need to move forward.

*Attitude* has so many meanings. There is attitude in the way that you sit, walk and stand—your posture. Are you upright, sitting up straight or slouching? Are your shoulders square when you walk? Attitude can be your feeling or emotion toward something. In ballet, it is a dance position. In modern jazz, it is a dance excitement. In flight, it is the way that an aircraft is positioned in the air, along vertical, horizontal and longitudinal axes (up and down, side to side, front to back).

When a plane makes its ascent, the take-off and the period just after take-off require more energy and effort than the flight. The pilot must keep the plane steady from all angles as the plane encounters different elements of nature from pressure to moisture. The pilot must keep a certain attitude on the plane so that it is safe and passengers can have a smooth flight. It has to be kept steady in its forward movement, even when it turns; that is longitudinal attitude. It has to be kept steady as it rises through the air; that is its vertical attitude. Its wings have to be kept steady; that is the horizontal attitude. Once the plane is above the clouds and with a good pilot of course, the ride is smoother under a clear sky and it requires less effort to sustain a smooth flight.

Just as a plane can be attitudinized to take you above the clouds for a smoother flight, you can take yourself ‘above the clouds’ by attitudinizing yourself in a positive direction. A plane is built for forward movement and you are built for forward movement. A pilot is responsible and accountable for the attitude of the airplane. He/she attitudinizes the plane for effective forward movement. You and I are the pilots of our journeys and experiences.

As you move forward in your life, there may be many circumstances that need to be adjusted. They can range from relationships to physical actions. They may be immediate or long term. In addition to attitudinizing yourself, you can attitudinize your circumstances in a positive direction. For example, I was driving a long distance home one day. I was 200 miles away when it started to snow heavily. As it accumulated, I had to drive much slower and follow in the tracks of large trucks to keep moving forward, as well as attitudinize myself for my mental forward movement. My direction of success was to arrive home safely.

Above the clouds: smoother flight, easier control of attitude for forward movement and clear sky

You develop attitudes about the things that you see and experience. Those attitudes translate into thoughts, most times in fractions of seconds. When the raw thoughts occur, you can either take action, wait to hear more or let them go. Should you decide to take action, that is, make a decision or even speak, that is the time to translate your thoughts and your attitude(s) into the language of Consistent Positive Direction. For example, someone is standing in the '15 items or less' checkout in front of you at the supermarket with at least 20 items and you're standing there waiting with only two items. Your immediate thought may be, "That's not right. He's not supposed to be in this line." After you have given yourself the courtesy of hearing *your* thoughts, you can translate them to say, "He should be more considerate." That is attitudinizing yourself in a positive direction. If someone is with you, you can share your thoughts and attitude in the language of Consistent Positive Direction, whatever your feelings. You can *always* say what you mean *and* be genuine.

More examples:

**Attitude/thought:** It's a lousy day.
**A translation:** Today has got to be better.

**Attitude/thought:** Nobody ever listens to me.
**A translation:** I need someone to listen to me.

**Attitude/thought:** I'm sick and tired of traveling.
**A translation:** I really want to be home more often.

The human experience has thousands of examples. You have thousands of examples. You can always attitudinize yourself in a positive direction, still making your point, still being yourself.

Whatever thought reaction a person has to something that is said or done, the first step is to use the Positive Direction attitudinal **RITE**. This is the sequence that you can use to attitudinize yourself in a positive direction.
**R**eceive the information openly–an excellent opportunity for TOLLING
**I**nterpret the information openly. Listen to yourself.
**T**ranslate your interpretation(s) into a positive direction.
**E**xpress your attitude in a positive direction, to your- self and, when necessary, to others.

Remember. Listen to yourself *first* then translate into the language of Consistent Positive Direction. You can express attitudes in a positive direction in any situation. When it becomes automatic, your positive direction attitude evolves into your 7th Sense Attitude (your automatic sense of positive direction).

Conversations that really matter can vary in intensity. When you are on the same team, live in the same house, or interact in any way with other people, you can experience differences. There are times when you must work through differences because it matters. TOLLing and Attitudinizing yourself in a Positive Direction are the skills that help you to work through those differences and create the circumstances that need to be in place.

When differences exist in a conversation, they are opportunities for learning. By filling in the learning space between differences, you can learn other approaches, reconcile attitudes, understand and allow different thinking styles to work together. I call using this learning space the *Spatial Special*: taking the opportunity to *respect, resolve and/or reconcile differences*. It is another aspect of Spatial Respect in which you give others and yourself the respect to learn how to support each other in a positive direction.

**Spatial Special: The Power to Learn**

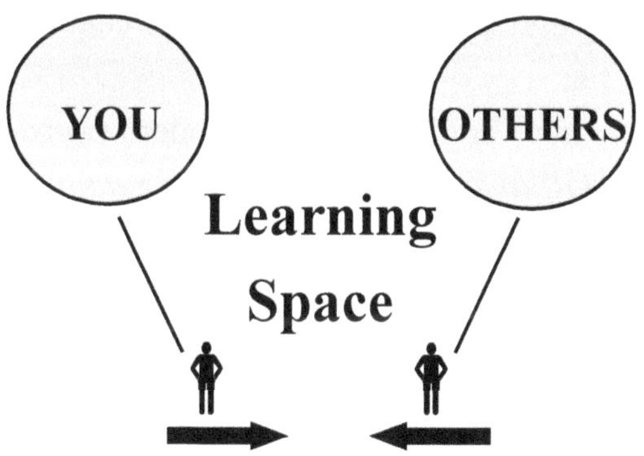


***to Respect/Resolve/Reconcile Differences***

Conversational learning in a positive direction can be quite powerful and successful, even if only one person uses the skills.

Therefore, conversations that really matter in an attitudinizing context are conversations that contribute to supporting and encouraging each other. To best support others, learning about differences should be a part of the process. The differences could be different or opposite attitudes, approaches and/or thinking styles. They can either be extreme, lightweight or somewhere in between.

There comes a time when the plane must land. When it descends through clouds and weather, once again it requires more effort to attitudinize the flight, until it arrives safely on solid ground. So, take yourself above the clouds, take your team above the clouds, take your organization above the clouds and make it work *on solid ground*, where you live, where you work, where you fulfill your purpose. *Make your positive direction attitude work on solid ground.*

Your positive direction attitude is a skill; your everyday attitude is a feeling. Even though your attitudinal feeling may stay, you can put your positive direction attitude to work right away. Whatever your feeling, whatever your mood, you can always use Consistent Positive Direction in your speaking, writing, learning and in expressing your attitude. Remember your Attitudinal **RITE**.

Once again, here is your skill reminder. *Consistent Positive Direction is a skill to speak in a positive direction rather than to be positive. Positive direction is the direction of the required and desired results, accomplishments, achievements, goals, objectives and/or successes. It can be a full glass or an empty glass, forward or reverse, up or down, one side or the other.*

Now go and practice your positive direction attitude. Remember. If your attitude about something or someone is in an 'other than positive' direction, rearrange the *direction* of the attitude rather than the attitude itself. You are well equipped.

# CONCLUSION

Congratulations on completing *Your Positive Direction NOW*. The purpose of this book was to provide you with a solid start on skills and approaches that you can use for the rest of your life. The emphasis is on *direction*. This sets the foundation to advance your skills in two ways. The first is practice. You know you can practice with every sentence that you speak or write. The second is to learn more about Consistent Positive Direction.

This book is an enhanced version of the first three chapters of my book *Taking Charge of Your Positive Direction*. The subsequent chapters in the book give you deeper knowledge and richer experience that you can use immediately. You can learn more details for your personal and professional life about using the Opportunity Models for Action, creating and managing reality and attitudinizing yourself in a positive direction.

Some of the advanced skills and approaches in *Taking Charge of Your Positive Direction* are called **Power Options**. They are approaches for many of the verbal and written encounters that we have in our lives. Many of them connect to what you already know. With the infusion of Consistent Positive Direction, they are connected to human experiences, stories and observations. Hence, you will encounter a number of approaches that are titled with acronyms or phrases such as 'Inside RAPPP', 'LEAPS and REAPS', 'The Silent Mentor', 'EPIC Toughness' and more. You have already experienced TALKEASE. You will learn more applications for TOLLing. There are over 180 Power Options. Those that are included in *Taking Charge of Your Positive Direction* expand your readiness for forward movement, resolving differences, finding solutions, building relationships, and making change work more easily, all in a positive direction.

This book was written so that you could start using the skills and approaches right away. As you practice you get better. With your new-found skills, your strongest level of mastery is everyday conversation. When you use the skills all of the time, you will always use them when you need them most.

# APPENDIX
## GENERIC EXAMPLES OF VERBAL POSITIVE APPROACH

**Instead of: can't or cannot be or [do something] … if**

**You can say:**

| | |
|---|---|
| can be … if | could be … if |
| might be … if | If … then … can be … |
| The is best to… | It is best to… |
| can work, if … | What can …? |
| How can …? | What is the best way to …? |
| Who can …? | When can …? |
| Where can …? | It is best to find someone else … |
| It is better … | The best … |
| The only … | The highest … |
| The lowest … | The maximum … |
| The minimum … | The farthest … |
| The closest … | The earliest … |
| The latest … | The biggest/largest … |
| The smallest … | The widest … |
| The most narrow … | The easiest … |
| The softest … | The hardest … |
| The lightest … | The heaviest … |

The best way it can [be/do/happen] is … if …

**Instead of: can't or cannot [happen], if …**

**You can say:**

can [happen], if …

can [happen]

Who/what/when/where/How can …

**Instead of: couldn't or could not …**

**You can say:**

See phrases under can't or cannot [happen], if…

**Instead of: couldn't or could not [understand] …**

**You can say:**

only understood …

Everyone understood but me.

needed more information to understand

needed a better or (different) explanation to understand

Wanted to understand, however …

could have (or would have) understood it better if…

Someone else should have explained.

**Instead of: didn't or did not …**

**You can say:**

All [I] did was …

I only did …

I should have done …

No. (In answer to a question)

**Instead of: difficult or hard [to do]**

**You can say:**

need to work at it

takes some effort

put time into it

takes practice

you can do it

will get comfortable with it

requires a lot of energy

The best way …

put a lot into it to be successful if you work at it

**Instead of: disturb**

**You can say:**

Comfort (able) excuse me …

… quiet …

… privacy …

**Instead of: [don't] disappoint…**

**You can say:**

Make it successful …

You can do it …

Make [it] work.

Be successful.

Do it correctly.

Good luck …

**Instead of: disappointed in/that …**

**You can say:**

expected more …

really thought that …

really wanted …

just knew that …

trusted …

What happened?

wanted to believe …

expected [you] to …

really believed that …

really expected …

hoped that …

Why …

felt that …

**Instead of: Don't or Do Not [do something]**

**You can say:**

It is best to …

The best …

The highest …

The maximum …

It is better …

The only …

The lowest …

The minimum …

| | |
|---|---|
| The farthest … | The closest … |
| The earliest … | The latest … |
| The biggest/largest … | The smallest … |
| The widest … | The most narrow … |
| The easiest … | The softest … |
| The hardest … | The lightest … |
| The heaviest … | Only do … |
| The best thing to do is … | Do [something else] |
| You know better than … | Do [the opposite] |
| Wait! Before you do … | Do what you are supposed to … |

**Instead of: doesn't or does not…**

**You can say:**

| | |
|---|---|
| only does… | does… |
| Does…? | The best… |
| The only… | The highest… |
| The lowest… | The maximum… |
| The minimum… | The farthest… |
| The closest… | The earliest… |
| The latest… | The biggest/largest… |
| The smallest… | The widest… |
| The most narrow… | The easiest… |
| The softest… | The hardest… |
| The lightest… | The heaviest… |

**Instead of: Don't/do not [go…..]**

**You can say:**

Stay…

Go [somewhere else]

The best way to go is…

Wait until…

**Instead of: Don't or do not [understand] or have a clue**

**You can say:**

need to understand

clarify or please clarify

Help me to understand…

know very little about…

…would like to understand

Let me see if I understand…

Let me be more clear…

All [they] understand is…

**Instead of: not allow/not allowed**

**You can say:**

only allowed…

The only way that…

**Instead of: No matter [who, what, when, where, how]**

**You can say:**

Whoever, whatever, whenever, wherever, however

**Instead of: fear or afraid**

**You can say:**

…Courage…

…calm…

Feeling that is needed or you would like to have

**Instead of: 'hurt' (emotional)**

**You can say:**

| | |
|---|---|
| thought that… | expected… |
| really felt… | needed to trust… |
| wanted to trust… | had a lot of faith in… |
| really wanted… | was really important… |

If only you knew/realized…

thought that [I] could depend on…

**Instead of: I don't care (opinion)**

**You can say:**

It's all the same to me.

It's ok with me.

Whatever works.

**Instead of: I don't care (feeling)**

**You can say:**

[Be quiet instead of using the phrase]

The only thing I am concerned about is…

It still has to be done.

**Instead of: I don't know**

**You can say:**

| | |
|---|---|
| The only thing I know is…. | All I know is….. |
| If you find out, let me know | I'll/I will find out |
| [He/She] is a stranger to me. | This is the first I knew… |
| I wish I knew | I would like to know |
| This is the first I heard about… | I am hearing this for the first time… |

**Instead of: I don't like...**

**You can say:**

I prefer...

I like it better if.....

The only thing I like is...

No thank you.

It would be better if...

I'd rather have something else...

**Instead of: I didn't want/need...**

**You can say:**

It would be better if...

What I really want/need is...

would be more comfortable if...

What is the best way to...?

**Instead of: lack or lack of...**

**You can say:**

needs...

needs more of...

needs more...

should / must have...

**Instead of: isn't or is not...**

**You can say:**

Is...?

The best...

The only...

The highest...

The lowest...

The maximum...

The minimum...

The farthest...

The closest...

The earliest...

The latest...

The biggest/largest...

The smallest...

The widest...

The most narrow...

The lightest...

The heaviest…
The softest…
The lightest…
The easiest…
The hardest…
The heaviest…

**Instead of: liar…**

**You can say:**

expected the truth…
How can I trust…?
will have to prove yourself…
can only trust you if…
should have been truthful…

**Instead of: lie…**

**You can say:**

truth…

trust…

**Instead of: never…**

**You can say:**

always…

From now on…

This is the first time that…

**Instead of: not [doing]…**

**You can say:**

only [doing]…

could / should / would be [doing]…

**Instead of: Not only [this] but…**

**You can say:**

in addition to…
besides [this]…

**Instead of: [this]…not [that]…**

**You can say:**

[this] rather than…

[this] instead of…

[this] in place of…

**Instead of: problem**

**You can say:**

issue

equation

resolution… [needed]

need or the need is…

situation

happening

solution… [needed]

what should be happening

**Instead of: ridiculous**

**You can say:**

A [much] better way to…

Is there a better…?

The best thing to do is…

Wish it would…

Think!

The best way to handle it is…

Wish it were…

Have a better idea.

**Instead of: [calling someone or something] stupid/dumb…**

**You can say:**

what about…?

need a better [idea]…

Let's talk.

a much better way…

know better…

What were you thinking?

Think!

Did you know about?

**Instead of: uncomfortable…**

**You can say:**

Need to be more comfortable…

would be more comfortable with/if…

**Instead of: ...won’t or will not [do something]**

**You can say:**

It is best to…

The best….

The highest/lowest…

The farthest…

The earliest/latest…

The smallest…

The most narrow…

The softest…The hardest…

My ‘plate is full.’

I will do [it] if…

What I am doing now is…

It is better…

The only…

The maximum/minimum…

The closest…

The biggest/largest…

The widest…

The easiest…

The lightest… The heaviest…

The only thing I will do is…

Someone else will have to do it…

# Bibliography

Ajzen, I., Fishbein, M., (1980). Understanding attitudes and predicting social behavior. Upper Saddle River: Prentice Hall.

Alessandra, T., O'Connor, m.J. (1998). The platinum rule. New York: Warner Books.

DuPraw, M. E., Axner, M. (1997). Working on common cross-cultural communications challenges. Promfret: Study Circles Resource Center.

Freeman, J. (2005). Taking charge of your positive direction. Vancouver: Trafford Publishing.

Kirton, M.J. (1989). Adaptors and innovators. New York: Routledge.

Maltz, M. (1960). Psychocybernetics. Engelwood Cliffs: Prentice Hall.

Marzano, R.J. (2003). What works in schools: translating research into action. Alexandria: Association for Supervision and Curriculum Development.

Maslow, A.H. (1987). Motivation and personality, 3rd ed. New York: Addison-Wesley Educational Publishers.

Nathan, A. (1999). Everything you need to know about conflict resolution. New York: Rosen Publishing Group.

Sedmak, N.J., Vidas, C. (1994). Primer on equal employment opportunity. Washington, D.C.: The Bureau of National Affairs, Inc.

Thomas, R.R., Jr. (1991). Beyond race and gender. New York: AmACOm.

Townsend, D.J., Bever, T.G. (2001). Sentence comprehension: the integration of habits and rules. Cambridge: mIT Press.

Ueshiba, M., translation by Stevens, J. (2002). The art of peace. Boston: Shambala Publications.

www.ingramcontent.com/pod-product-compliance
Ingram Content Group UK Ltd.
Pitfield, Milton Keynes, MK11 3LW, UK
UKHW041930190726
13854UKWH00004B/1538